The
Awkward Squad

Chris Hudson

RMEP

RELIGIOUS AND MORAL EDUCATION PRESS

The
Scale Model

T he ship's hold stank. Oh no … he was going to be sick!
Thomas quickly scrambled back up the ladder to get a few
breaths of fresh air.

'Sorry about that!' the ship's doctor whispered from
underneath. He was below deck at the foot of the ladder, staring
up and looking worried. 'I forgot to warn you about the stink.
We get used to it, you see. Quick! Get back down here before
someone notices you!'

Thomas held his breath, then climbed back down the ladder
into the hold, dreading the moment when he would have to
open his lungs again and take in the awful stench. He tried it,
coughed, then gradually started breathing normally, trying to
think of anything else that would stop him from feeling sick –
but it was difficult. The air was thick with a foul odour.

'Do you think *this* is bad?' muttered the ship's doctor. 'You
should smell it when it's *full*!'

'Tell me about it,' replied Thomas, taking out his notebook
and pencil, 'I want to know everything.' As the doctor began to
speak, Thomas started to write furiously.

'Well, in this hold they fit in about four hundred and fifty
bodies. You look surprised? Sometimes they can fit in two or
three times that number! They put them in lying down, allowing
each one a space of about four foot by one foot. Sometimes it's
less. Remember that they have to be chained as well, to stop
them running about! They stay in that position for the whole

3

voyage, except when we bring them up on deck to have a little exercise and fresh air.'

'What about fresh water and food?'

'That gets lowered down in buckets for them, and the food is often just a cold vegetable stew. It's not enough, I keep telling the captain that, but he says that he can afford to lose a few of the weak ones because he can sell the fit ones at such an amazing profit. He says that they're just creatures, after all, and they don't feel pain the way we do. Sometimes, we've lost half of them through disease. The bodies just get thrown overboard.' He paused, picturing it, then added. 'We see a lot of sharks following us sometimes.'

Thomas turned angrily on him. 'What do *you* think? You're the ship's *doctor*! You should know if a living creature can feel pain.'

The other man paused, then spoke. 'Yes, I think they *do* feel pain. At night, we can hear all sorts of awful noises coming up from the hold, especially when we're going through bad weather. Most of the crew say they've felt uneasy about it at times, but for them it's just a job. They're only following orders. They all have families to support in Bristol. Somebody has to pay their wages, and for many of them, it's either this or join the Navy, and only an idiot does that. "A man's got to live." That's what they always say – a man's got to live.'

'Do *you* say that?' Thomas stared hard at the doctor, who looked away, embarrassed. Thomas felt angry with him, then sorry for being so rude – the man was helping him after all, and he could lose his job just for showing Thomas around the ship. But what was that he said? 'A man's got to live?' Thomas gazed around the hold, his eyes now used to the darkness.

You wouldn't keep cattle in these conditions! So why were they treating people like this? Innocent men, women and children were being captured, bought and sold like cattle, chained up and dragged away from their native lands in Africa, to be forced to

The triangular trade

The African (or Bristol) Trade worked in a triangular pattern, with some ships working all three of the routes. Slaves were taken from Africa to America, and cash crops were taken from America to Britain and the rest of Europe. Goods were then produced in Britain and Europe to sell or exchange for slaves in Africa. Neat, wasn't it? Slavery made a great deal of business for so many people …

work as slaves in the sugar plantations of Jamaica. Thousands died during the crossing. Families were torn apart, husbands separated from their wives and parents torn away from their children. It was all incredibly cruel, but no

Slavery now

Slavery still exists today! You can find out more from Anti-Slavery International on **www.antislavery.org/** and from the Anti-Slavery Society on **www.antislaverysociety.addr.com/** and **www.childlabor.net/**

one in England seemed to care – after all, it made the country rich and produced the sugar that everyone liked to stir into their tea. But it had to stop! The whole awful business had to stop!

Thomas felt helpless. What would it take to convince people that the slave trade was barbaric? How could he convince people that the whole filthy business was *wrong*? Nobody would believe him. He stared around the ship's hold again in disgust. How many people had died forgotten in this floating dungeon? How many tears had been shed? This was an evil place, but few really knew about it, and those who did, didn't seem to care. How could he make decent people sit up and listen and *care*?

Then all of a sudden, he had an idea. He picked up the notepad and started drawing. He took some rough measurements, pacing up and down and then jotting down the numbers on a diagram that quickly took shape. If only he'd brought a measuring stick! Oh well, this would do for now. The ship's doctor was curious at this change in behaviour.

'What are you doing? I thought you only wanted to write down everything I said.'

'I'm making some sketches.'
'What for?'
'You'll see.'

'No one shall be held in slavery or servitude; slavery and the slave trade shall be prohibited in all their forms'

Article 4, Universal Declaration of Human Rights

6

Later that day, Thomas set to work in his study. He took out some large sheets of paper and started making sketches of the inside of the ship. Let's see … he'd have to think about getting the exact sizes right, so he'd need help from someone who understood ships and scale, and he might have to make another visit, to check that the measurements were as exact as possible.

How big was the whole ship again? How many slaves did it carry? All the details would have to be exactly right.

A few weeks later, Thomas invited the ship's doctor round to his house. 'I've got something to show you!' he said grinning proudly, holding something up to the light.

'A model ship?' asked the doctor, taking it in his hands and looking a little puzzled. 'That's something the old sailors make for a hobby! It's a bit big. What's all this about? I thought you had your mind on higher things!'

'I have. Look closer!'

Taking the model back, Thomas set it down on the table, fiddled with some catches and took the main hull of the ship apart, in layers. The doctor studied the model closely.

'Oh … *now* I see.' He gave a low whistle.

It was a scale model of the slave ship, designed to open out into parts that showed each of the decks in detail. Hundreds of slaves were shown lying down in the hold, chained to the floor, packed together like peas in a pod, with no space to move – just as they were in real life. If you could have taken a real slave ship apart, then this is what it would have looked like. The doctor was impressed.

'What are you going to do with it?'

'I'm going to send it to a friend. Have you heard of William Wilberforce?' The doctor nodded. 'He's planning a campaign with me. We're going to put a stop to this buying and selling of human lives. This model will show people the truth about what a slave ship is really like inside. It might take years, but we'll do it, because it's right and God is with us. It'll be a long fight, but in the end, we'll win. We'll do it by persuading people, telling them what's going on, showing them the truth about the slave trade – and as our Lord said, the Truth will set people free, all over again.'

He held part of the model up to the light, and looked closely at the little bodies huddled up together on one of the decks.

'Yes,' he muttered. 'One day, they'll see.'

The scale model

This scale model was created to convey the sheer awfulness of conditions on a slaver ship. It still remains a powerful image. Remember – the slave trade was all about making money. Each slave arriving safely in the Americas could be worth thousands of pounds in today's money.

A time-line for slavery

1444 Portugal first imports slaves from Africa.

1496 Christopher Columbus brings back 'Indian' slaves to Portugal from America.

1510 King Ferdinand of Spain approves sale of African slaves in America.

1672 King Charles II of England approves setting up of Royal African Company for slave trade.

1772 Slavery abolished within England. (No *English person* allowed to be a slave.)

1778 Slavery abolished within Scotland. (No *Scottish person* allowed to be a slave.)

1780 By this time, about 70 000 African slaves were being taken across the Atlantic to America *every year*.

1783 Clarkson and Wilberforce's 'Committee for Effecting the Abolition of the Slave Trade' formed.

1807 Slave trade abolished by Britain and its colonies.

1833 Slavery itself abolished in British colonies.

1839 'British and Foreign Anti-Slavery Society' formed, aiming to abolish slavery throughout the world (now called 'Anti-Slavery International').

The long struggle

Thomas Clarkson was born in 1760, did well at school, and went to college in Cambridge. He was a rising star: in 1785 he wrote a prize-winning essay entitled 'Is it lawful to make men slaves against their will?' Then his life changed, on a journey to London. He was trying to find a publisher when he says he 'had a vision'. God had told him to devote the rest of his life to abolishing the slave trade. Clarkson went on to London and found a publisher. Meanwhile, a 'Committee for Effecting the Abolition of the Slave Trade' was being formed, including such names as William Wilberforce MP, John Wesley (the Methodist preacher) and Josiah Wedgwood (of pottery fame). Clarkson joined them and became the campaign researcher.

He journeyed to slaving ports such as Liverpool and Bristol, carried out hundreds of interviews and produced masses of evidence. The campaign took a long time. The Slavery Abolition Act wasn't passed until 1833, but it gave all slaves within the British Empire a new level of freedom. Clarkson retired to Ipswich, where he died in 1846. Without him, British slavery would have continued for much longer. His success also turned the British Navy into a powerful force for good – its West Africa Squadron began to hunt down slave ships and set their prisoners free. Slavery still continued in the USA until the end of the American Civil War in 1865, and in Brazil until the 1890s. *It still exists now.* To find out more, see 'Slavery now' on page 6.

Slavery in history

'Slave: a person who is the legal property of another or others, and is bound to absolute obedience.'
(*Oxford Encyclopedic Dictionary*)

Slavery has existed for thousands of years in many different forms. In biblical times, it was an organised way of keeping servants, but slaves could always choose to leave a master after a number of years. In Roman times, you could (if you were lucky) pay your way out of slavery to become a freedman. (Most of the gladiators who fought in the Roman arena were slaves or captured prisoners.)

Fighting back

Many black slaves played their own part in the battle against slavery. There were numerous slave revolts on land and sea, some of the most successful being on the island of Haiti, and on the ship *Amistad* (a story now filmed by Steven Spielberg). Also, many free black people helped to smuggle escaped slaves to freedom. Harriet Tubman later became famous for organising a whole network called the 'Underground Railroad' in the USA, with secret passwords and 'safe houses'. Some escaped slaves (including Oladah Equiano and Frederick Douglas) also published their own stories as part of the public campaign.

11

more

Making money

In the seventeenth century, slavery was seen as the only possible way to provide workers to grow cash crops like sugar, cotton and tobacco on the farms and plantations of America – and the best place to find workers who could cope with the climate was in Africa. Villages would be raided, prisoners would be taken, then marched to the coast. There they were sold on to traders who took them away by ship and sold them to landowners in America. Many Africans made a lot of money from this, as each captive was worth hundreds or thousands of pounds in modern money.

Some people (and ports like Liverpool and Bristol) also grew incredibly rich. They fought hard to keep it that way, just as modern dealers do to protect their trade in illegal drugs. About 10–13 million people were taken from Africa during that time period, never to return. We still don't know exactly how many suffered like this, and never will. Each one of those millions of people was a person just like you and me.

Missionaries

Some of the unsung heroes and heroines of this time were the missionaries who went out to teach the slaves about Christianity, and who also sent back secret information from the plantations to Clarkson. (Many are still remembered with great affection in the Caribbean.) They were blamed for 'giving the slaves ideas' and organising slave revolts. Slave owners did not like the idea of slaves becoming Christians, because it meant that the slaves were human beings just like themselves. Some missionaries even sold *themselves* into slavery, so that slaves could hear about Jesus! Christianity is sometimes seen as the religion of the oppressors. But here, it wasn't!

The Final Treatment

Elder Long was so pleased! It was a sunny day, perfect for everything that he had been planning. The football stadium was filling up, and there were lots of policemen watching the crowd. Long gave a nod to the director of music, and the band began to play cheerfully. Soon, the Dancers of the Revolution would come out to perform for the crowd as the band played, weaving their ribbons and flags in a swirl of exciting colourful patterns. Long had spent a great deal of money on these dancers and musicians. It was all worth it, now. It *had* to be.

He gazed around the impressive stadium and smiled. Yes, this was what it was all about. There were red flags everywhere, with yards and yards of bunting flapping in the stiff breeze. He felt proud to be Chinese, and proud to be part of the Revolution in Yunnan province. Today would be remembered as *his* day. The Party leaders always said that the Party would reward 'acts of outstanding service'. Today would convince them.

Long sat back in his chair. He could almost relax now, because it was all going to plan. The crowd

13

China – the sleeping giant?

The people of China were ruled by powerful emperors and warlords for thousands of years. The Chinese invented many new products such as gunpowder and paper, but some of their leaders were suspicious of 'change'. By the 1800s, they were being outclassed by other modern countries that could create things like medicine, steamboats or rifles. China was thought to be a very 'backward' place: attractive to look at, but behind the times. In the Victorian era, some Western traders in China actually started and encouraged a massive trade in opium (a powerful drug), creating thousands of Chinese addicts! They were even supported by the British Navy, who fought the Chinese government when they tried to stop it! Things like that aren't forgotten quickly.

How China changed in 1949

During the Second World War against Japan, many Chinese decided it was time to rebuild their country from scratch. This led to a revolution in 1949 and a new government for 'The People's Republic of China'. Their new message could be summed up as: 'If it's not Chinese, it's bad.' Foreigners were sent home, and anything 'foreign' was attacked, including religions introduced by foreigners such as Christianity, Islam and Buddhism. These attacks grew worse in the 1960s, during the time called the 'Cultural Revolution'. A lot of people ended up dead or in prison as the Chinese government and its student supporters (the Red Guards) tore their country apart, looking for enemies to blame their problems on! That's where Elder Long got started ...

were clapping along with the music and enjoying the dancers, who were now performing on a big stage at the centre of the football pitch. This was the way ahead, he thought – with music and dance and colour. Give the people this, and they won't need *anything* else. They won't need religion any more.

He had come a long way himself. He remembered all the time he'd been at religious college, training as a Christian minister. It now looked so stupid, but it had been useful, because it showed him how the enemy worked. These Christians fooled people with all their talk of a loving God who cared. Huh! It was just a smoke-screen to keep the poor from seeing the truth and asking awkward questions! China was different now. The Revolution was sweeping away all these lies.

He'd realised that on a tour of Beijing, on a summer's day in 1951. He was taken to see the Imperial Temple of Heaven and shown the famous Echo Wall. The Emperors had used the Wall to make their voices sound like those of the gods when they spoke to the people – but it was just a clever trick using sound waves and a smooth surface that made a human voice sound weird. He'd even tried it out for himself. 'LISTEN TO MY VOICE, I SOUND LIKE A GOD!' he'd said in a deep voice, with the echo bouncing around the hall. That's how people get fooled, he thought. That's how religion works – it's all a trick! He decided he wasn't a fool, and left the college. Now he was a keen supporter of the local Communist Party in Sapushan district.

He knew the truth now. People didn't need God. It was as simple as that. If they wanted to put some colour into their drab lives, they went to church. But now, he would give them something better. He would provide concerts of music, theatre and dance. The people just needed a bit of 'culture', not religion.

Of course, it hadn't been as simple as that. Superstition is like an infectious disease or a cancer – sometimes it has to be cut out. He knew that now. Elder Long felt he was like a surgeon holding a sharp scalpel, cutting out all the crazy ideas that kept people stupid. Every time he burned a Bible or put another church leader in prison, he knew he was doing more good, and making China more fit and healthy. Today would be the *final* treatment.

They had rounded up all the Christians in Sapushan district and brought them to the stadium. They had a leader called Wang Zhiming, but he had already been arrested, put on trial, then sentenced to death for being an enemy of the Revolution. Elder Long

The 'surgeon'

Elder Long was a church member until the 1960s, when he joined the 'Red Guards' – the student groups who supported the 'Cultural Revolution'. The police often just stood by and let them get on with wrecking someone's house or burning all the 'wrong' books in a library. People like Elder Long were allowed to do whatever they wanted. He was put in charge of the 'irreligious model' experiment, to see if people could be steered away from religion by providing other things for them to do, like going to the theatre. It didn't work. He was still furious about this when someone interviewed him about it in 1988! (What's more, he didn't think the government was grateful enough for all the good things he had done!)

had been there when the sentence was read out in court. What a victory! The Red Guards had cheered and clapped. But it wouldn't be enough to execute Wang Zhiming in prison where no one would see it. Something like this would have to be done in public, in front of all the people that Wang Zhiming had fooled with his stupid lies about a

Persecution: subjecting a person to hostility or ill-treatment, especially on political or religious grounds.

God who cared. Then they would *see* what happens to liars. If you cut off the disease at its root, then the disease would die.

The chief of police came over to where Long was sitting. 'The crowd are getting restless, sir. I think you'd better do something.'

Elder Long frowned. The programme of music and dance was only halfway through, but never mind. 'Very well. Bring out the prisoner.' He barked out some orders, and the Dancers of the Revolution were sent back to their places, looking slightly confused. Then with a roll of drums, the band started to play some new music, the Chinese national anthem. Everybody rose, standing to attention – and then the prisoner was brought out.

'It's Wang!' he heard someone shout. A few people started to applaud, but the policemen stopped them. The prisoner was brought out to stand on the platform, facing the place where Elder Long and his officials were sitting. Wang Zhiming was surrounded by a lot of guards, but he didn't look particularly dangerous. In fact, he looked rather frail. That's the way it is with liars, thought Long. You can't see how dangerous they really are. He rose and stepped up towards his microphone.

'Wang Zhiming,' he shouted, 'you have been arrested, tried in the people's court, and found guilty of being an enemy of the Chinese people! Your lies have twisted the minds of hundreds of good, decent folk, and you have been sentenced to death. Is there anything you wish to say to the people before the sentence is carried out?'

The old man nodded and stepped forward away from his guards towards a nearby microphone. Elder Long smiled. This whole speech had already been agreed with Wang, who had asked that his family's lives be spared if he could just say three things to the crowd. Long listened, then agreed. He couldn't see anything dangerous in Wang's final message, once he'd heard it. Let him speak.

Wang coughed, then spoke clearly into the microphone.

'I will tell the people what I have said to my own family. Firstly, you should not follow my example. Secondly, you should follow the words from above and repent once again. Thirdly, in all of your work, you should pay attention to cleanliness.'

Some of the crowd started applauding when they heard this, which sounded odd to Elder Long. Hadn't Wang been confessing to spreading all those lies about God?

The police chief turned to Long. 'Did you agree that little speech with him?' He nodded, but the police chief frowned. 'I just hope we don't regret it!'

'Why?'

'Look at them!' He pointed over at the crowd on the other side of the stadium. Some of them were actually waving at Wang Zhiming as he was taken down to the place of execution. 'You and I know what we heard, but I think it meant something else to that lot over there!'

Elder Long wasn't sure. 'Let's get on with the sentence,' he ordered. Wang was made to kneel by the executioner. He held his hands together in prayer, said something to the executioner, then bowed his head. The blow fell. Wang's body collapsed to the ground and lay still. At another signal from Long, it was dragged away by the guards.

'And so it ends,' muttered Long, signalling to the band, who started playing a cheerful march tune. But something was wrong – the crowd weren't sitting down. He could hear some of them shouting. Others were waving their fists. He was just sitting back

18

in his seat when he saw some women shoving past the guards and making their way across the pitch to where he sat. What was going on? The women weren't armed, but they looked furious.

'That was disgusting!' shouted one of them, pointing up at him.

'And you call yourself a leader of the people? A murderer, more like!' added another.

'Wang Zhiming never hurt a soul! He wasn't guilty of anything!' shouted another. 'You can keep your Revolution if it kills a good man like him!'

The police moved forward to arrest them, but stopped and looked around. More of the crowd were leaving their places and striding out on to the pitch. They were heading this way, and they outnumbered the police. Some were holding bits of wood that they'd torn down. Flags were being ripped up.

'Stop them!' shouted Long to the chief of police.

'It's too late for that!' he replied. 'You'd better leave now *while you still can*!'

He grabbed Long and hustled him through a door, down some steps and out of the stadium into a waiting car. It was nearly too late. Some of the crowd were pushing their way through the line of police to get at him, and even trying to throw a few punches! Long was bundled into the car by the chief of police – and with a screech of tyres, they were quickly driven away.

What had gone

The secret message

What was Wang Zhiming talking about in his final message? People in Yunnan still talk about it. Most of them say he meant this:

'Firstly, you should not follow my example.'
(Follow Jesus' example instead!)

'Secondly, you should follow the words from above and repent once again.'
(Do what God says, not these so-called people in authority!)

'Thirdly, in all of your work, you should pay attention to cleanliness.'
(Be good in every possible way!)

A dangerous enemy

Wang Zhiming had been a Christian since childhood, employed first as a school teacher and then as a church minister. The authorities considered him to be a 'model worker', until the 'Cultural Revolution' came in the 1960s. (See 'How China changed in 1949'.) Wang criticised the way that the authorities encouraged people to confess their own 'crimes' and produce names of other local 'enemies of the people'. He refused to 'name names', was listed as an 'enemy of the people', and finally arrested in 1969. He was murdered in front of a mass rally of 10 000 people in 1973, where this story takes place.

Blessed are you when people insult you, persecute you and falsely say all kinds of evil against you because of me. Rejoice and be glad, because great is your reward in heaven...!

Jesus, quoted in
Matthew 5:11–12

wrong? Long rubbed at the bruise on the back of his head as the car sped along the road. He couldn't understand it.

'We need to spend more money!' he muttered. 'We've got to show these people how foolish they are!'

The police chief turned round in his seat and glared. 'Excuse me, sir, but did you say your wanted to spend *more* money? Would you please tell me *who's* been paying those people to be Christians?' Long fell silent, because he knew the answer – *nobody*. It didn't make any sense at all. Some people just didn't know who their friends really were!

Find out more

Amnesty International also have a website detailing human rights abuses around the world. Visit them at www.amnesty.org.uk/

The statue

At Westminster Abbey in London, there used to be some spaces on the west front, an outside wall over a main door. In 1995, it was decided to put up statues of ten Christians who have died for their faith around the world. Wang Zhiming is the last one on the right. Find out more at www.westminster-abbey.org/tour/martyrs10-wz.htm

What happened next?

From the late 1970s, a new Chinese government decided that attacking religion wasn't working – in fact, there were more believers in places like Yunnan than before! Instead, they tried to make peace with the Christians and paid compensation to the families of those who had been mistreated. They even rebuilt church buildings and put up a memorial stone for Wang Zhiming! At its foot may be found the words: 'They will rest from their labours, for their deeds follow them.' He is still remembered with great affection.

However, the government still allow only official 'registered' churches to exist, and the leaders of unofficial 'house' churches are still arrested and put in prison. To find out more about the current situation, visit the Voice of the Martyrs website at www.every3minutes.com

Juggling Balls

Thunk! Thunk! Thunk! It sounded good. He decided to throw the juggling balls at the door again, catching them as they bounced off. Thunk! Thunk! Thunk! It was like hitting a drum. This was bound to get their attention – good!

A guard came to the barred window that faced out on a courtyard and glared. 'Hey! Stop! Be quiet!'

James wasn't in the mood to stop. 'Get me a prison officer!' he replied.

A prison officer appeared, looking angry. 'Why are you doing this?'

'Because I am bored! I have been in this cell for six months, and I am still not allowed to keep all my books in the cell! You only let me have them one at a time. Why? If you don't give me the books, then I have to find other things to do. Throwing balls is fun!'

'No,' the officer replied. 'You cannot have them.'

James smiled at this. 'The prison governor said I could have them. Your government and secret police said I could have them. Do you remember?'

'They have to be checked first.'

'You've *already* seen them! I'm not talking about books that I haven't had yet. I'm talking about books that have already been in this cell!'

'They are in Rangoon.' That was hundreds of miles away.

'RANGOON? That's silly! They don't take every book I read

all the way to Rangoon!' This was getting stupid. The officer was obviously lying.

'You cannot have the books.'

James shrugged. 'Oh well, I'll just have to carry on doing this, won't I?'

Thunk! Thunk! Thunk! The sound echoed along the corridor outside his cell, then out around the prison. He had three home-made juggling balls, constructed from empty soup packets tied up with tape. James knew he was being awkward, and he knew that the guards would soon come searching for them. His whole life was now a weird game of cat-and–mouse with these people. He stopped throwing, hid one ball inside a toilet roll, and another by tying it to his leg with an elastic band. The third he kept in his hand, playing with it, throwing it up into the air and catching it again.

At noon, three guards came to his cell. As they opened the door, James decided to be polite while he sat there, playing with the third ball. 'Do you have my books?' he asked.

'No.'

'Can I write down the names of the ones I want?' He wanted a collection of poetry by Rudyard Kipling, an encyclopedia and *The Imitation of Christ*, a book about living as a Christian.

'Yes.'

'Can I keep the juggling balls?'

'Yes.'

'Are you sure?'

'Yes.' James didn't believe them, but he put the third ball down to see what they would do.

As soon as he got up to leave his cell for his daily exercise and wash, a guard snatched the third ball. So *that* was how they wanted to play it! More guards came in to search for the other juggling balls, but found nothing. James thought about the ball strapped to his leg – he would be having a wash soon! They'd see it – then what? He thought fast, then decided to take a stroll around the yard behind the cell, where they couldn't see him. Then he quickly unstrapped the ball and buried it in the earth. He could always get it later. The time to wash came. As soon as he was locked back in his cell, he found the first ball in the toilet roll and started throwing it at the door.

Thunk! Thunk! Thunk! It was a lovely noise, like a drumbeat. A guard came to the window to see what was going on.

'Will you give me my books?' James asked him.

'No!'

Oh well … Thunk! Thunk! Thunk!

Clang! The door was thrust open by the guards again. James hurled the ball out of the door, over their heads into the main prison area. At least it would give the other prisoners something to talk about. Now the guards had *two* of his juggling balls.

Later that evening, a friendly guard came to the window to give a word of advice. 'Mister James. We have been told that if you keep on making a noise, then we are to stone you.' He brandished his catapult, the sort they used to hunt the rats that were such a pest around the prison, then went away.

That made James stop and think. Would they use catapults on him? Probably – but this was getting *stupid*! The Burmese government didn't follow *any* kind of rules – that's why he was here in prison in the first place. They just thought they could do whatever they wanted, and anyone in

Bible inspirations

During his stay in prison, certain verses from the Bible became very important to James. Here are some of them:

'You shall know the truth, and the truth will set you free.' John 8:32

'If anyone has material possessions and sees his brother in need, but has no pity on him, how can the love of God be in him?' 1 John 3:17

'He has showed you, O man, what is good. And what does the Lord require of you? To act justly and to love mercy and to walk humbly with your God.' Micah 6:8

Burma who disagreed was 'an enemy of Burma'. It was a stupid argument, but they would shoot or lock up anyone who didn't agree. James had come to Burma to challenge that, and so he was thrown into prison as well – but he could still make a fuss, even over a few books. He couldn't let them win, not even over this.

What should he do now? He thought about it all night. Should he bang on the door with his fists? That was the trouble with protesting – you have to see it right through to the end. James felt afraid, and in the darkness, he decided to pray.

'Dear God, give me the courage to make this action.
Give me the strength to persist in this action.
Give me the humility not to lose my temper.
Give me the wisdom to speak sense afterwards.'

A history of modern Burma
[Union of Myanmar]

1962 A military junta seizes power in Burma. (A military junta is a group of soldiers who rule the country. Nobody votes for a junta – they just rule the country because they are the ones with the guns.)

1988 The Burmese army kills thousands of people during student protests against the military junta.

1989 Protest leader Aung San Suu Kyi is placed under house arrest.

1990 There is a real general election in Burma! Aung San Suu Kyi's democracy party (National League of Democracy) wins 80% of the vote, but is not allowed by the army to take power. She has won an election without leaving her house!

1991 Aung San Suu Kyi is awarded the Nobel Peace Prize.

1996 The Burmese Government brings in a new law that makes it illegal even to *talk* about politics in public!

He decided. Yes, he would make his protest when the prisoners were lining up on parade outside. But he would only hammer on the door for one and a half minutes. That would be enough to make his point. He remembered the friendly guard's warning: what about the catapults? The blanket on his bed *might* give him some protection, but not much.

Morning came. The prisoners were taken out from their cells and lined up in front of the guards and the Prison Governor. He held his breath, raised his fists and began.

Bang! Bang! Bang! Bang! Bang! Bang! Bang! There were angry shouts, the sound of guards hurrying over – and then they started throwing stones through the window at him! It was like being in a hailstorm! James covered his head and body with the blanket to shield himself, and carried on thumping the door until the time was up. When he stopped, the stones stopped flying as well. There was a weird silence. He stepped over to the window to see what was going on – there was quite a crowd out there, including the Prison Governor! James caught the Governor's eye and smiled.

'Don't you know it's wrong to keep someone in solitary confinement?' he called out. 'Where are my books? You won't even say *why* I can't have them!' The Governor hurried out of sight, looking quite shocked. No one normally spoke to him like this.

Then an officer ran up to the window. 'Shut up!' he shouted.

People were listening, so James kept talking. 'Why? You keep *lots* of other people locked up like this all over the country! What about Min Ko Naing, the student leader? He's not a criminal, but he's been in prison for *ten years*! You lock people up, you forbid them to speak! All around the world, it's the prisoner's right to make complaints – but not here, not here in Burma! Explain to me why I can't have the books! Give me a reason! That's all!'

The officer grabbed his catapult, loaded it and aimed it directly at James' face.

James kept talking. 'It's not me I'm complaining for – it's for everybody in this country!'

The catapult fired, the pellet whizzing past his ear.

James still kept talking. 'Give me a reason *why* I can't have the books! I'm protesting because this is all *wrong*!'

He fell silent, and the crowd started to move away. He turned to look at the inside of his cell – the floor was covered in stones, gravel and dust. He looked out of the window again. The guards were fetching stones and piling them up nearby. More of them were carrying catapults. Some were carrying large sticks as well. This was *not* looking good.

What could he do? Make some padding from his blanket and spare clothing? Hide out of sight of the window? They could still come in through the door and beat him with their sticks. How far did he want to take this? He still had one juggling ball hidden away, as if *that* mattered. He could keep thumping the door – what would happen then? Noon came. Should he thump the door again? What did God want him to do – die? Everyone has to stand up to bullies, but when can you stop?

At noon, James was let outside again for his daily exercise and wash. He thought about the ball he had buried in the yard the day before. He would have to dig it up so he could get it back into his cell and carry on with the protest about the books. It was frightening.

'God, I am so scared,' he thought as he stood there, 'but I am *not* going to give in to these bullies! I am frightened, but I am *not* going to give up until they give me the books or give me a reason why they hold them back.'

Just then, a guard came to the yard. He held three books – the Kipling, the encyclopedia, and *The Imitation of Christ*. Fantastic! He handed them all to James, who was so pleased he felt like hugging the man! He took the guard by the arm and led him round the yard to the back of the cell. Then he dug up the last juggling ball and gave it to him, as a thank-you present. The guard stared, then burst out laughing. This round of the fight was over – but there would be others.

How it all began

When James Mawdsley was 13, a Burmese boy joined his school and they became best friends. Later on, when James heard about the pro-democracy leader Aung San Suu Kyi being put under house arrest in Burma, he was filled with admiration for her and felt that he wanted to support her somehow. He dropped out of university to travel the world, and later went to Burma to live at a rebel camp in the jungle, where he taught children English.

After that, the campaigning began. In September 1997, he took a journey into the capital city of Rangoon and made a protest outside a school. For this he was deported (thrown out of the country). He did it again in April 1998, and was jailed for 99 days. Then in September 1999 he did it again, and was sentenced to 17 years in prison. He was released in the year 2000 after a lot of pressure was put on the Burmese rulers by people around the world.

Universal Declaration of Human Rights

In 1948, the United Nations General Assembly agreed on a range of human rights that would set the standard for every government to keep. It has 30 Articles (paragraphs). Here are some of them.

Article 1
All human beings are born free and equal in dignity and rights.

Article 5
No one shall be subjected to torture or to cruel, inhuman or degrading treatment or punishment.

Article 18
Everyone has the right to freedom of thought, conscience and religion.

Find out more
James now works for Christian Solidarity Worldwide, an organisation that works to defend people around the world who are persecuted for their faith. For more information, visit their website at **www.csw.org.uk**

James' books

James' family were able to send him books, but the prison authorities made some strange decisions about what he could or couldn't have in his cell.

He was allowed to read:
Long Walk to Freedom, the story of Nelson Mandela's 26 years in prison.
One Day in the Life of Ivan Denisovich, a story about surviving life in a prison camp.
They Have Their Exits, a true-life story about escaping from prison camps.
Dying We Live, a collection of powerful letters from people in prison for their beliefs.
God's Smuggler, about smuggling Bibles past guards.

He was *not* allowed to read:
A Diskworld novel by Terry Pratchett. (Find a booklist and guess which one!)
Mr Brave and *Mr Uppity,* two stories by Roger Hargreaves about the Mister Men!

Work that out if you can!

Religious and Moral Education Press
A division of SCM-Canterbury Press Ltd
A wholly owned subsidiary of Hymns Ancient & Modern Ltd
St Mary's Works, St Mary's Plain
Norwich, Norfolk NR3 3BH

First published 2003

ISBN 1 85175 302 8

Designed and typeset by
TOPICS – The Creative Partnership, Exeter

Illustrations by David Johnson

Printed in Great Britain by Halstan and Co. Ltd., Amersham, Buckinghamshire
for SCM-Canterbury Press Ltd, Norwich